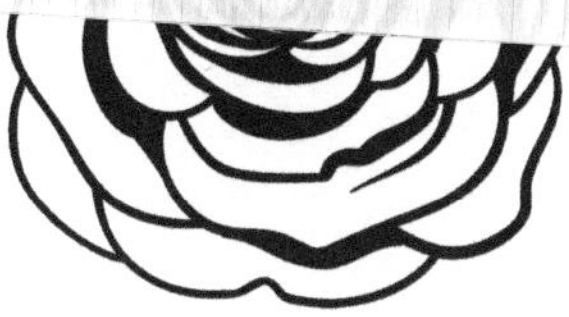

This book belongs to:

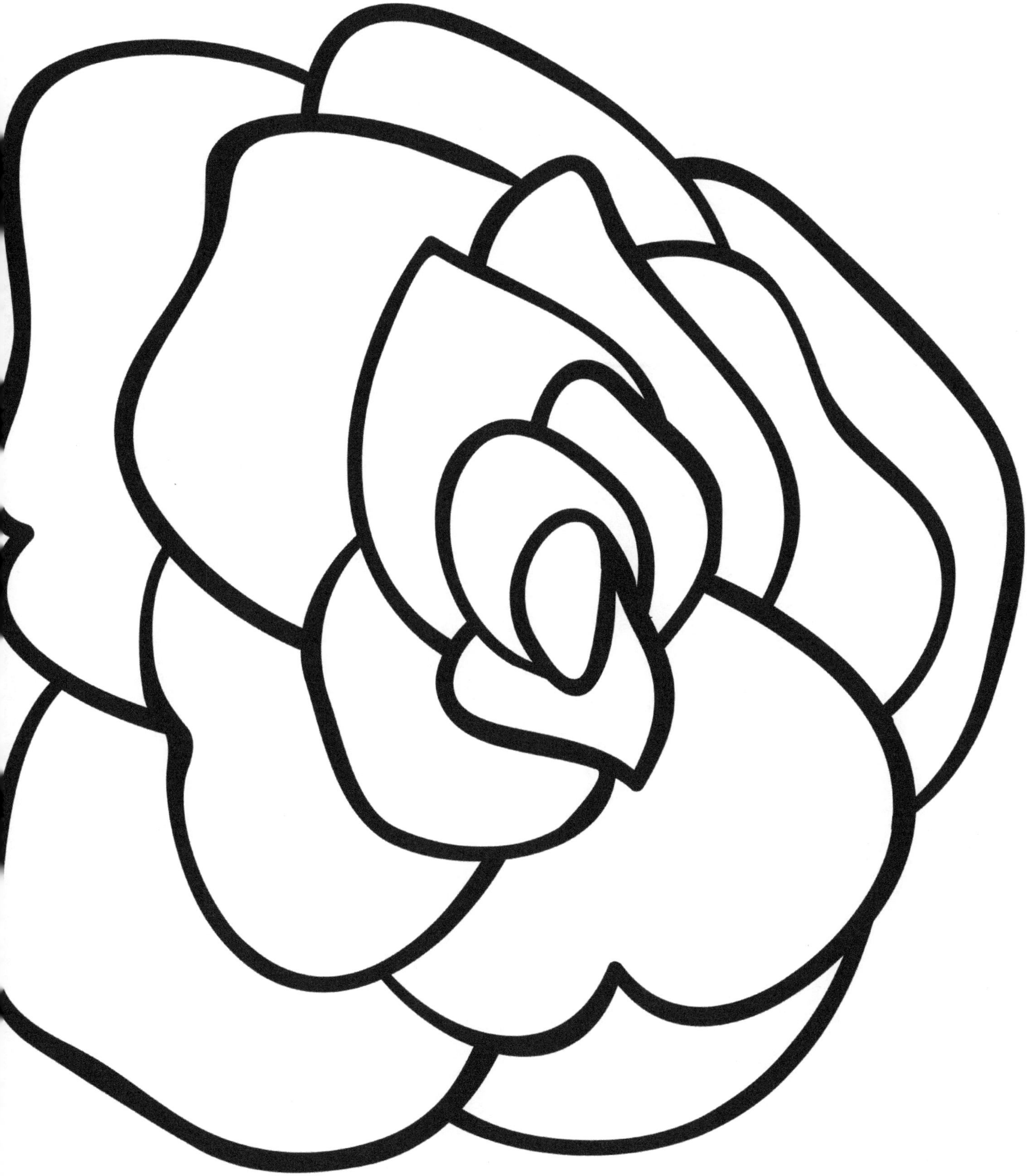

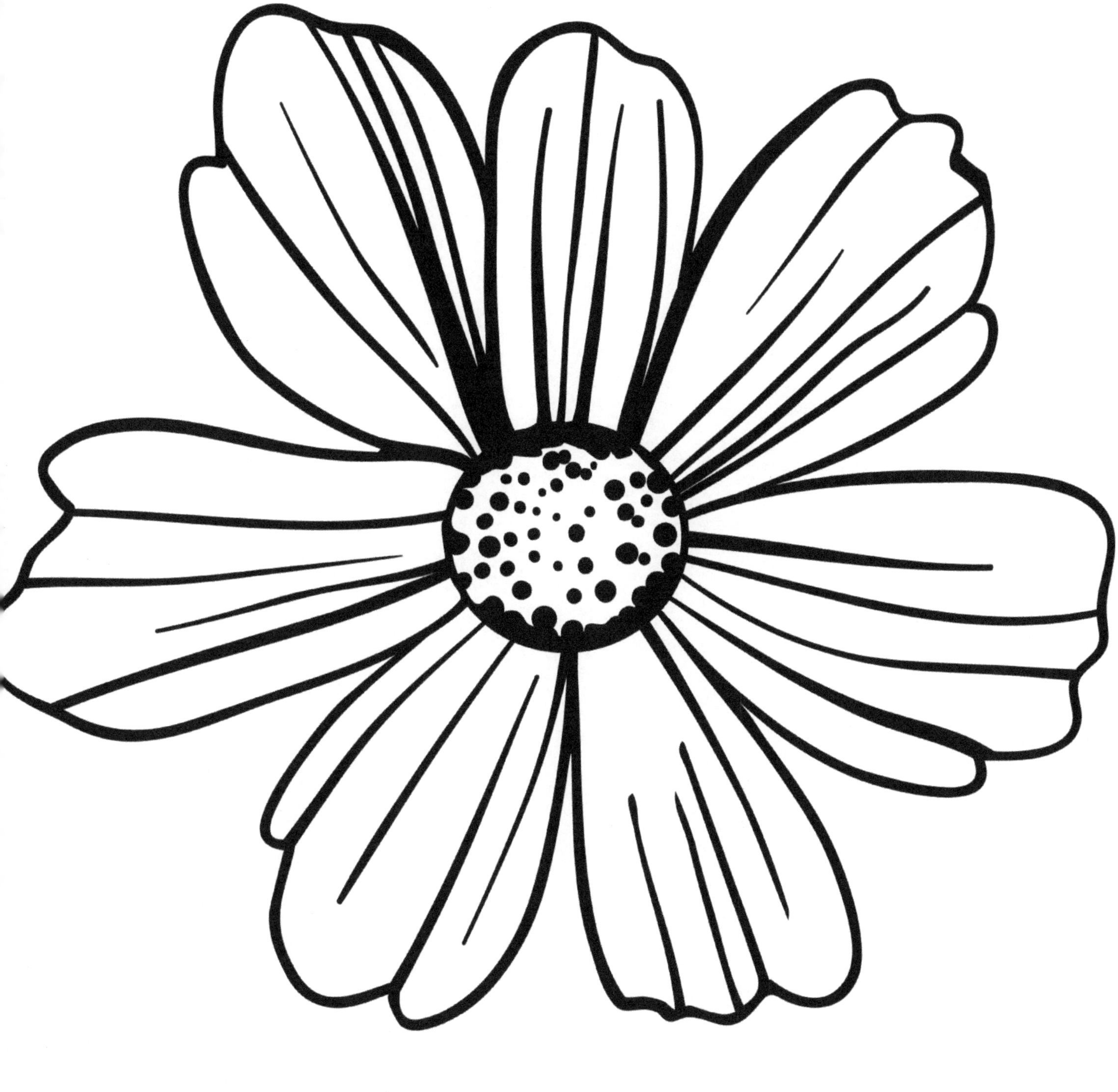

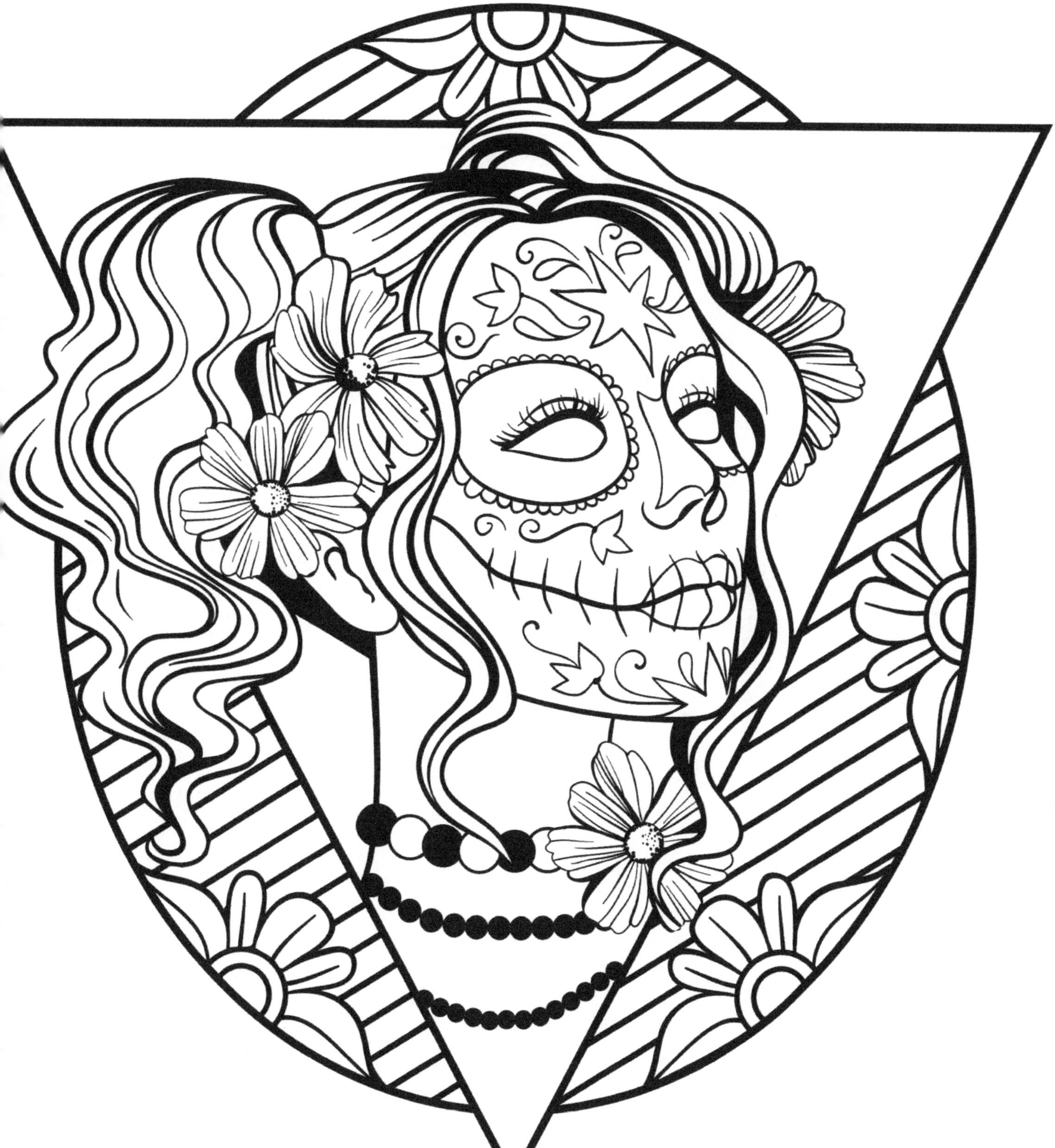

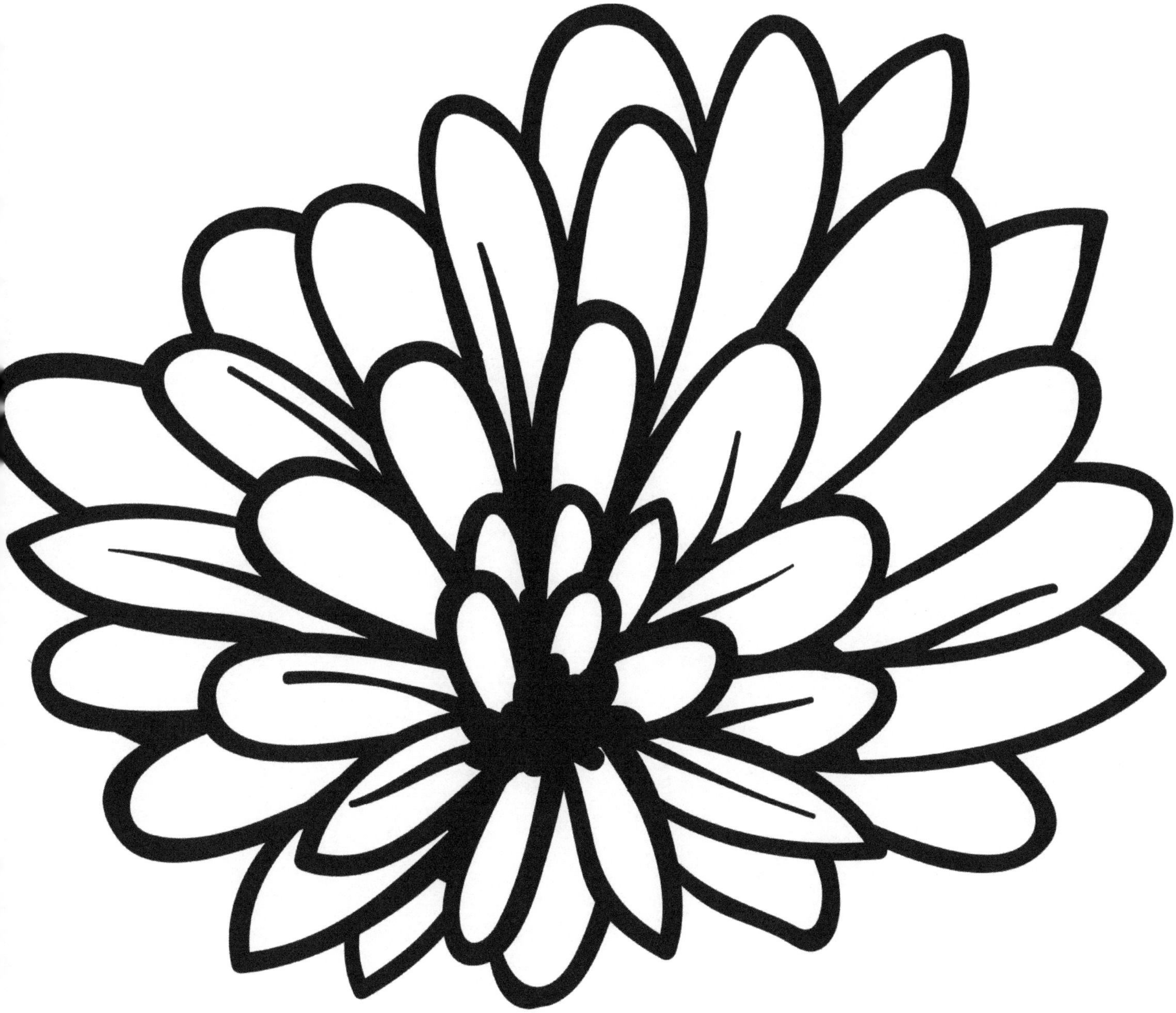

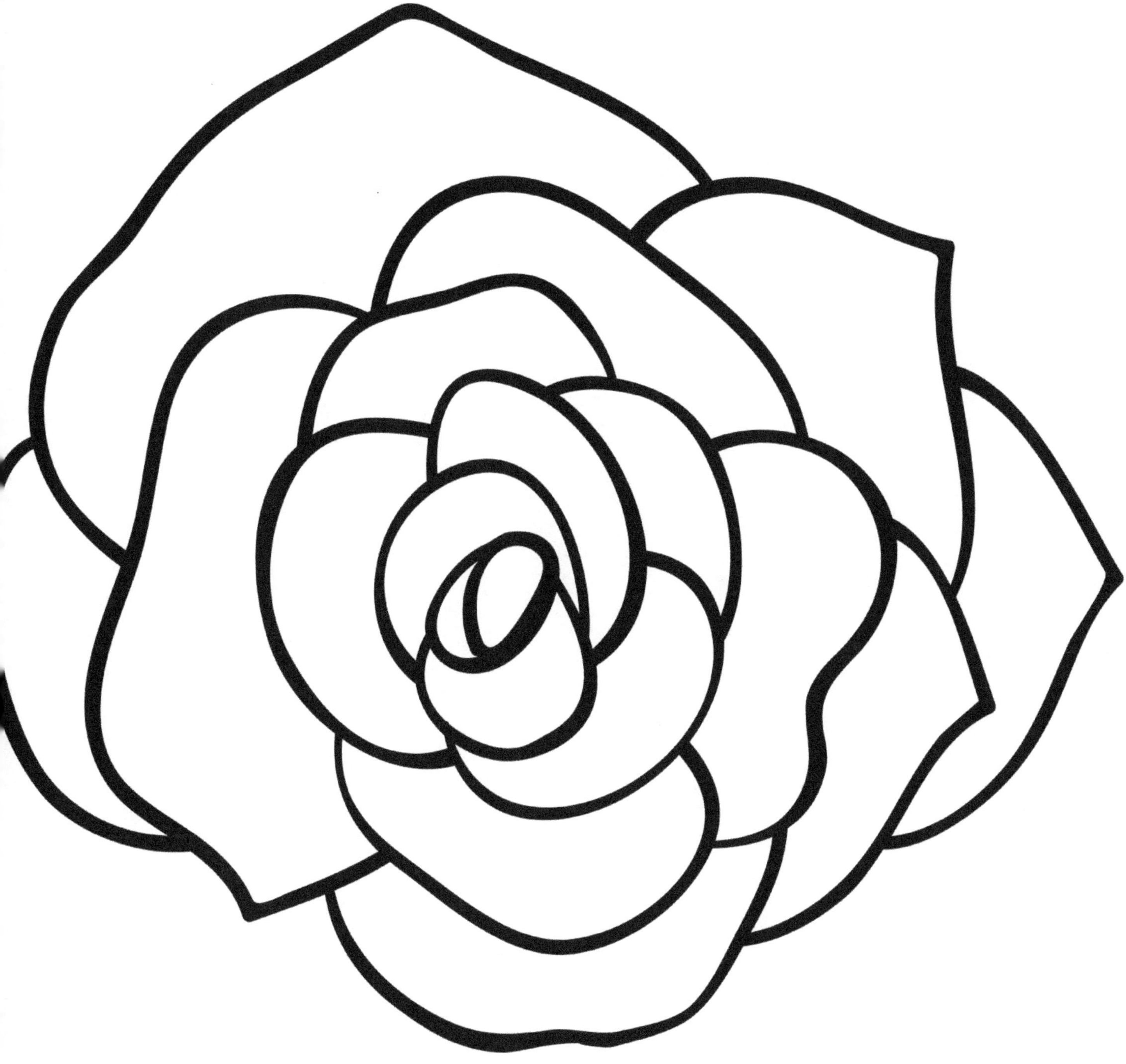

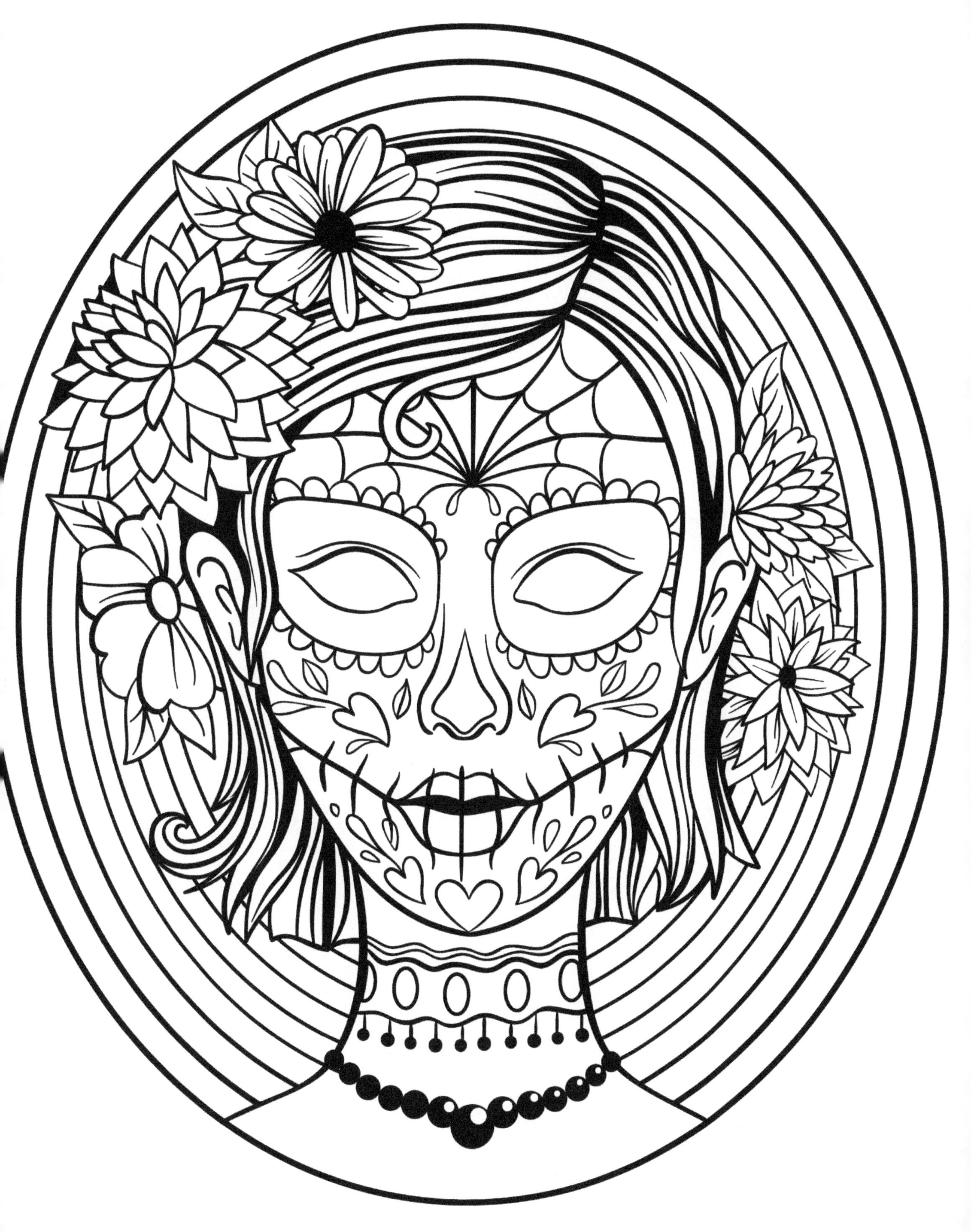

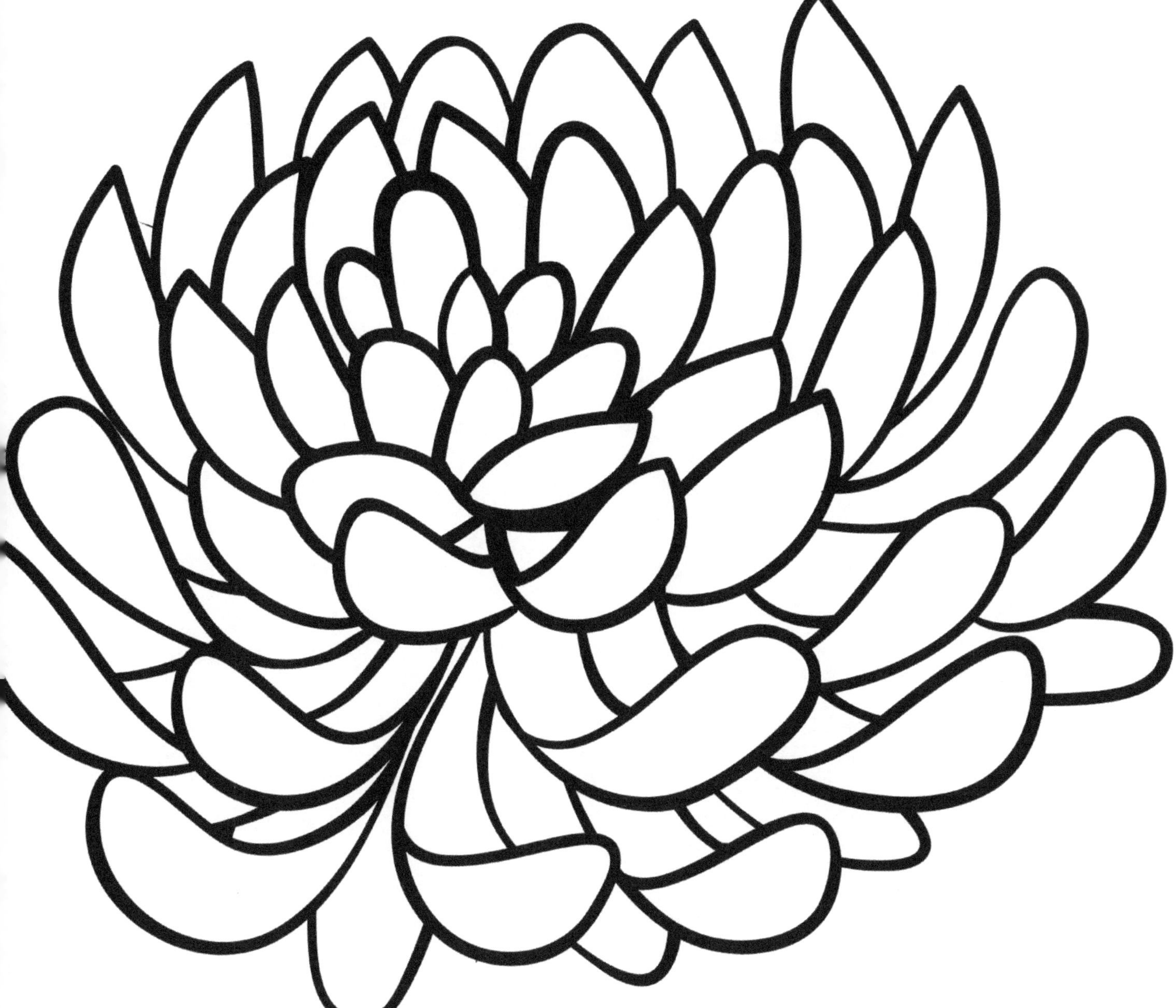

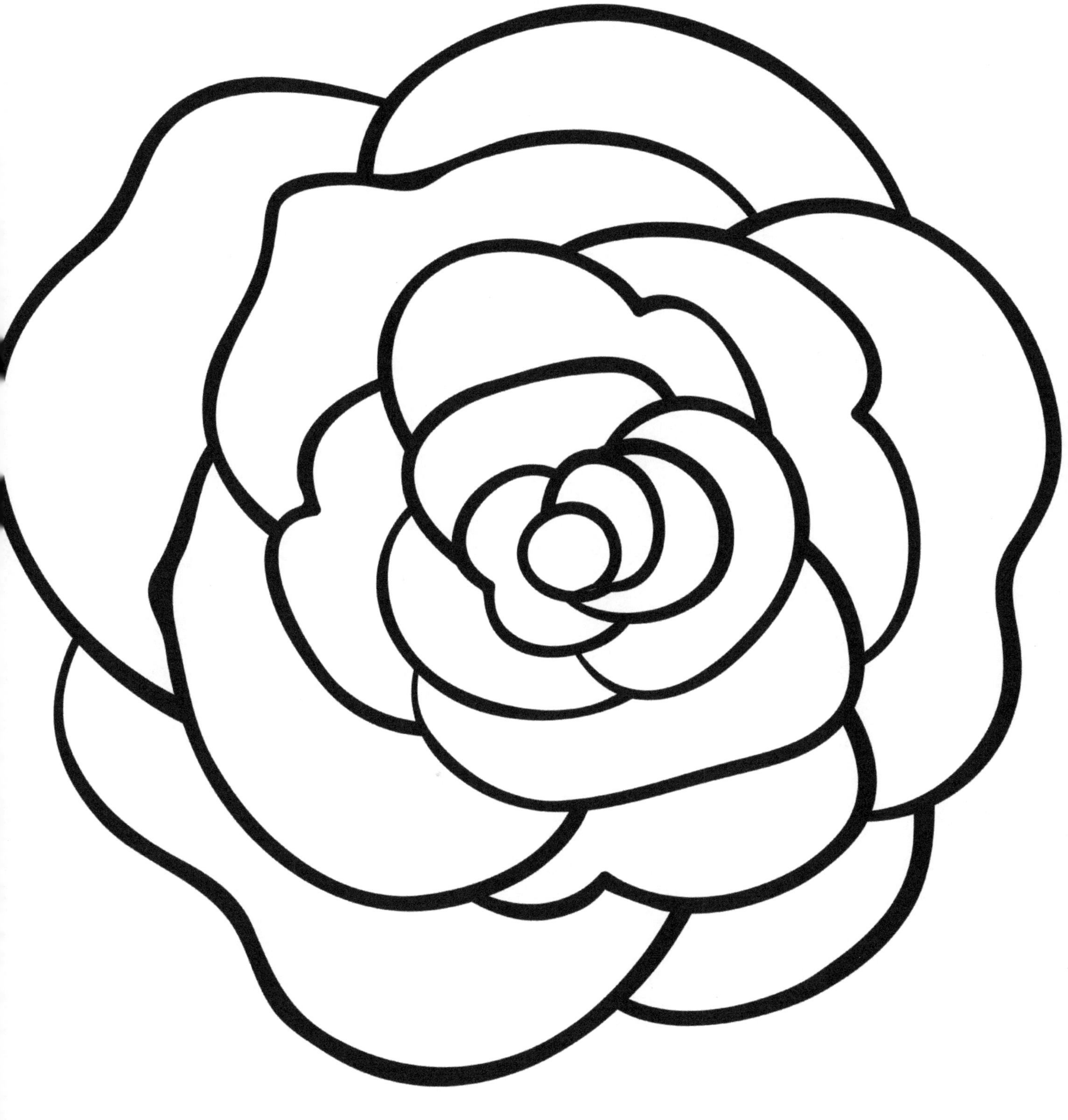

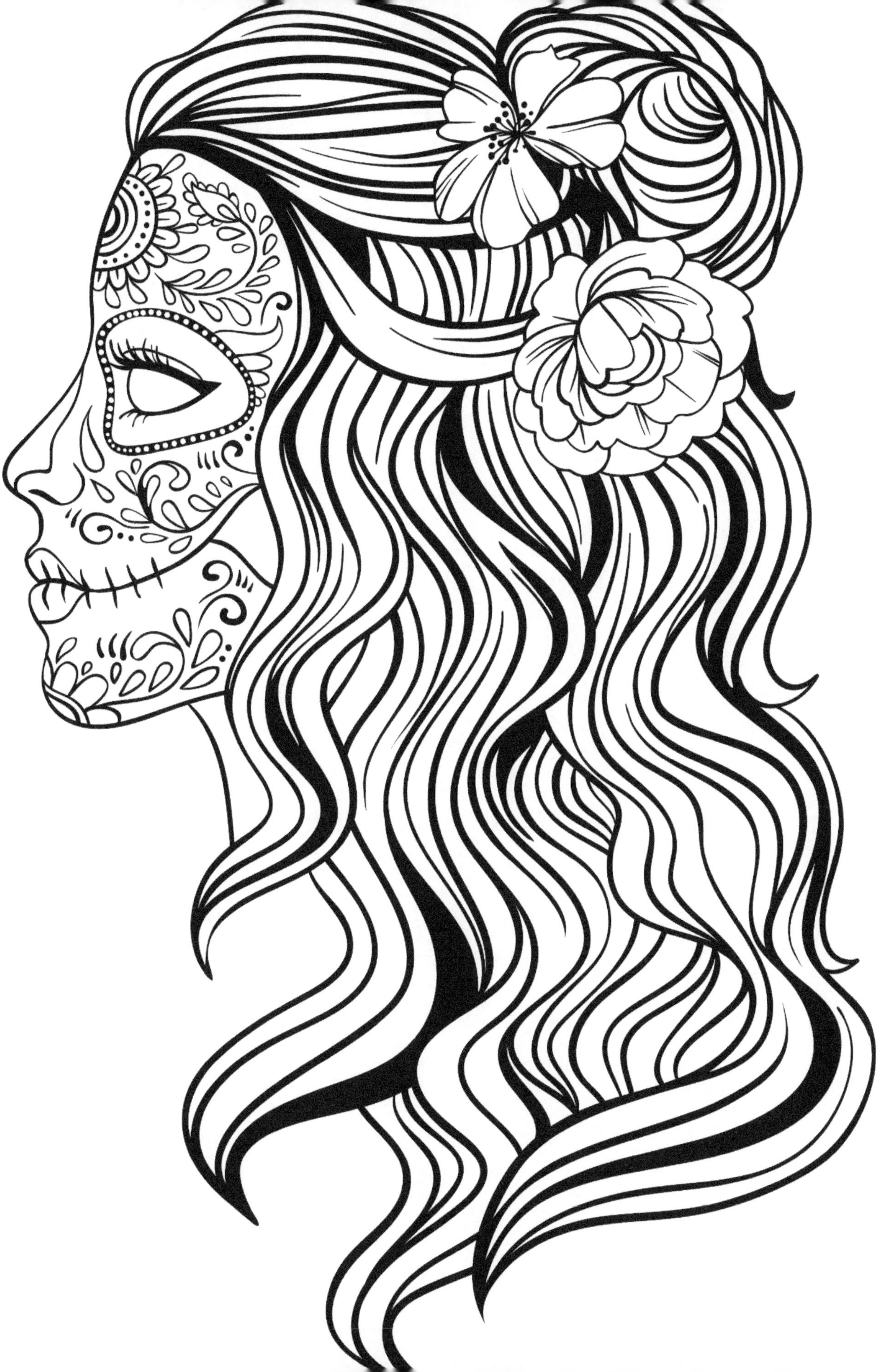

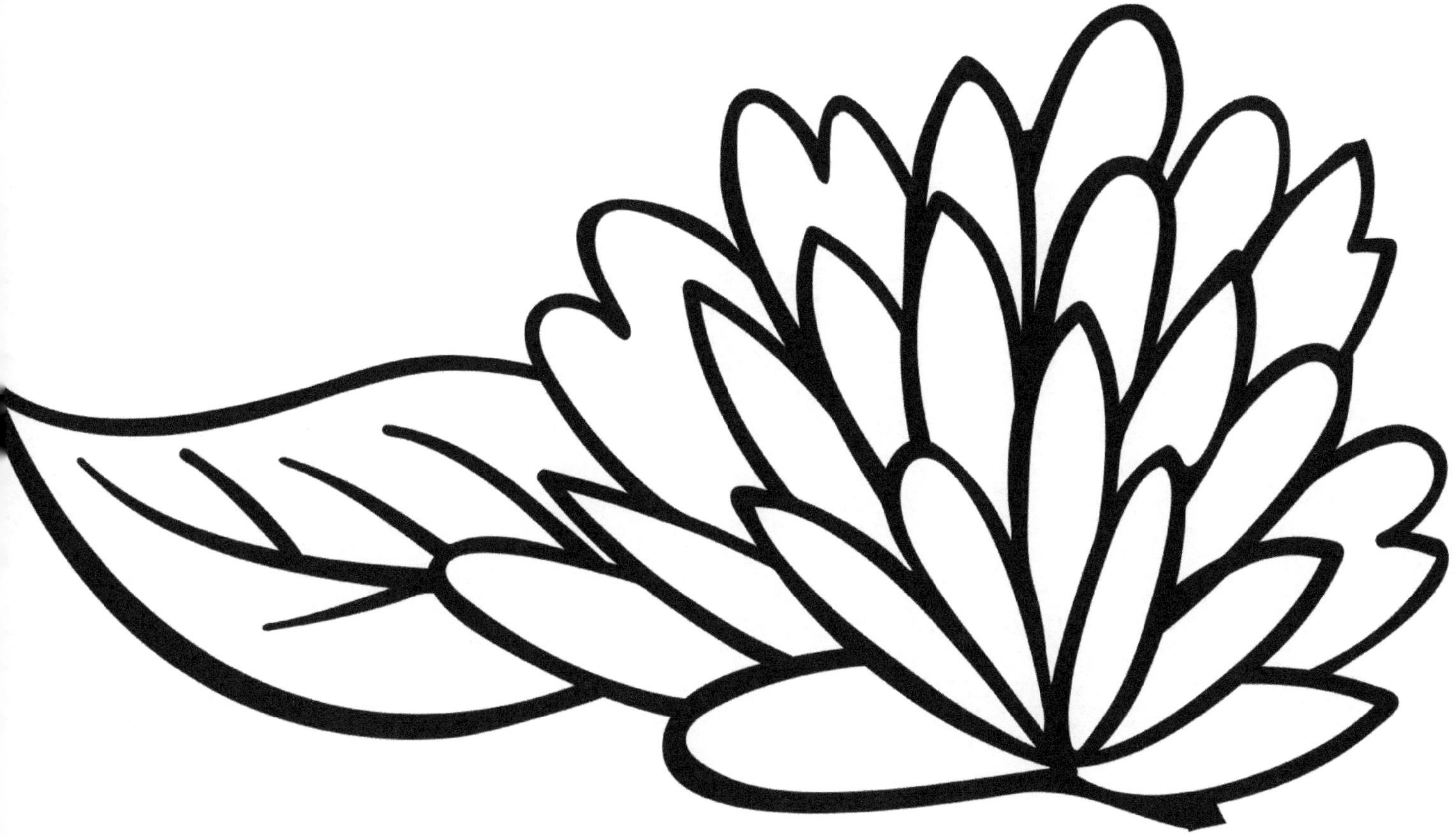

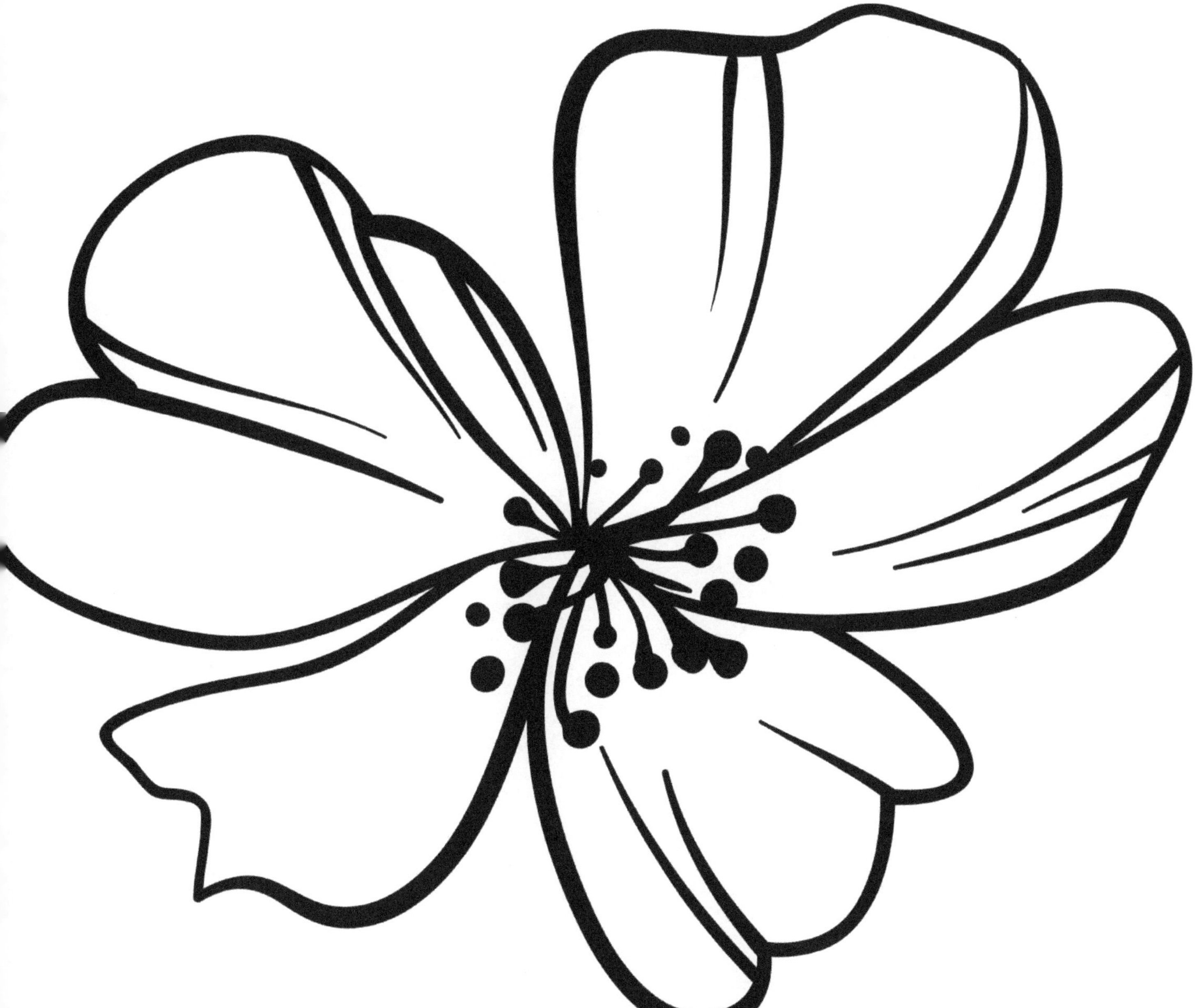

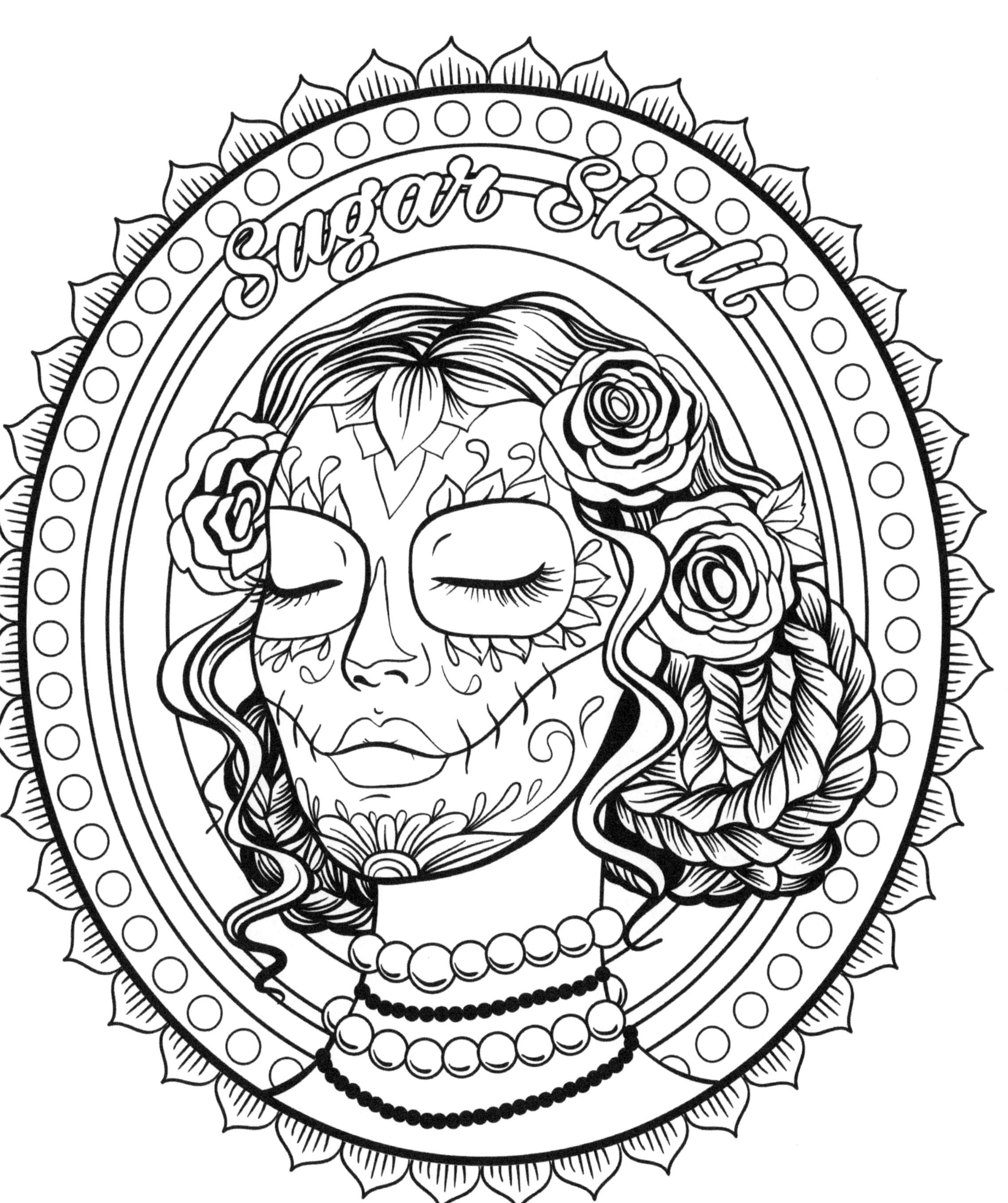
Sugar Skull

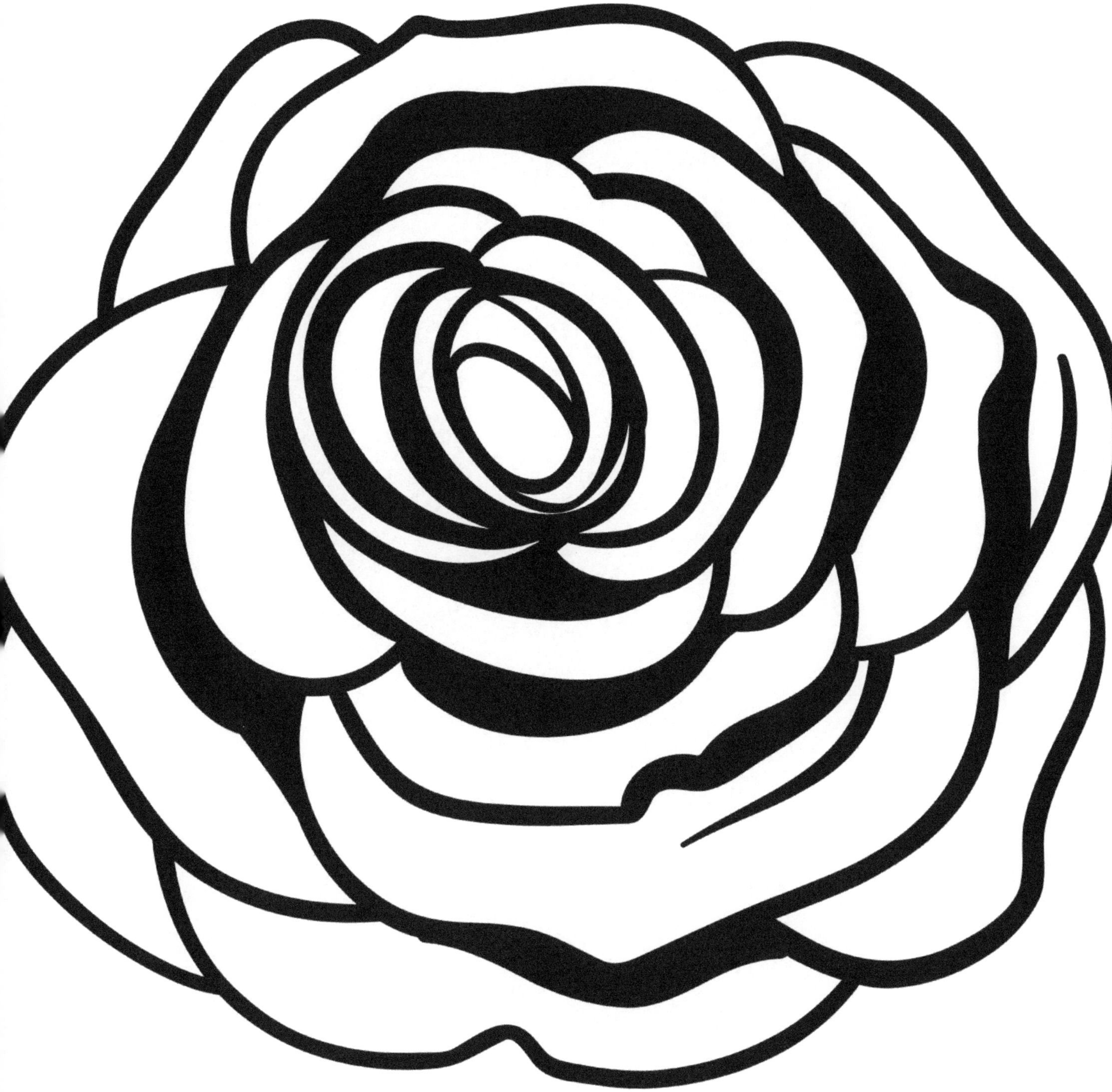

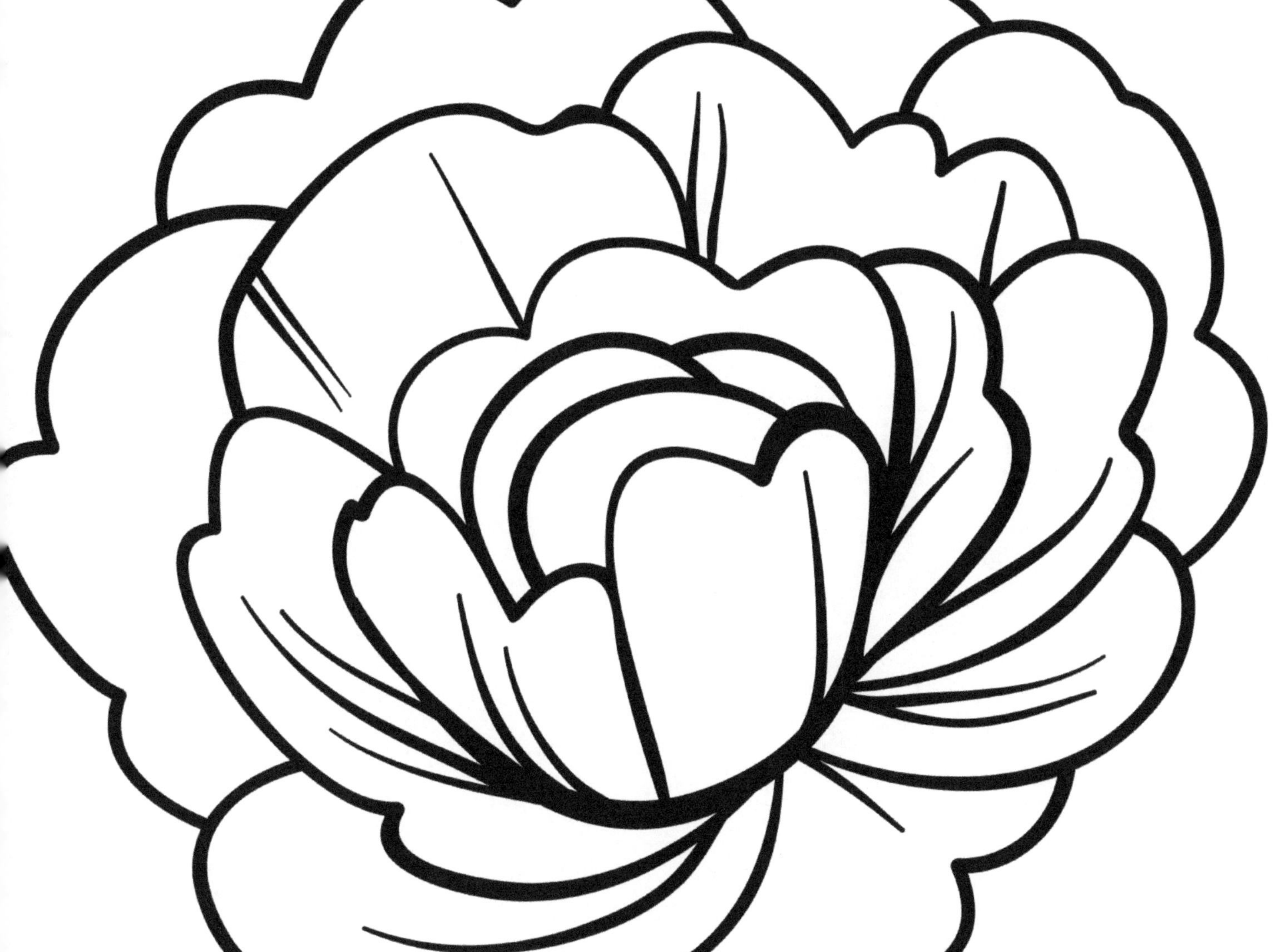

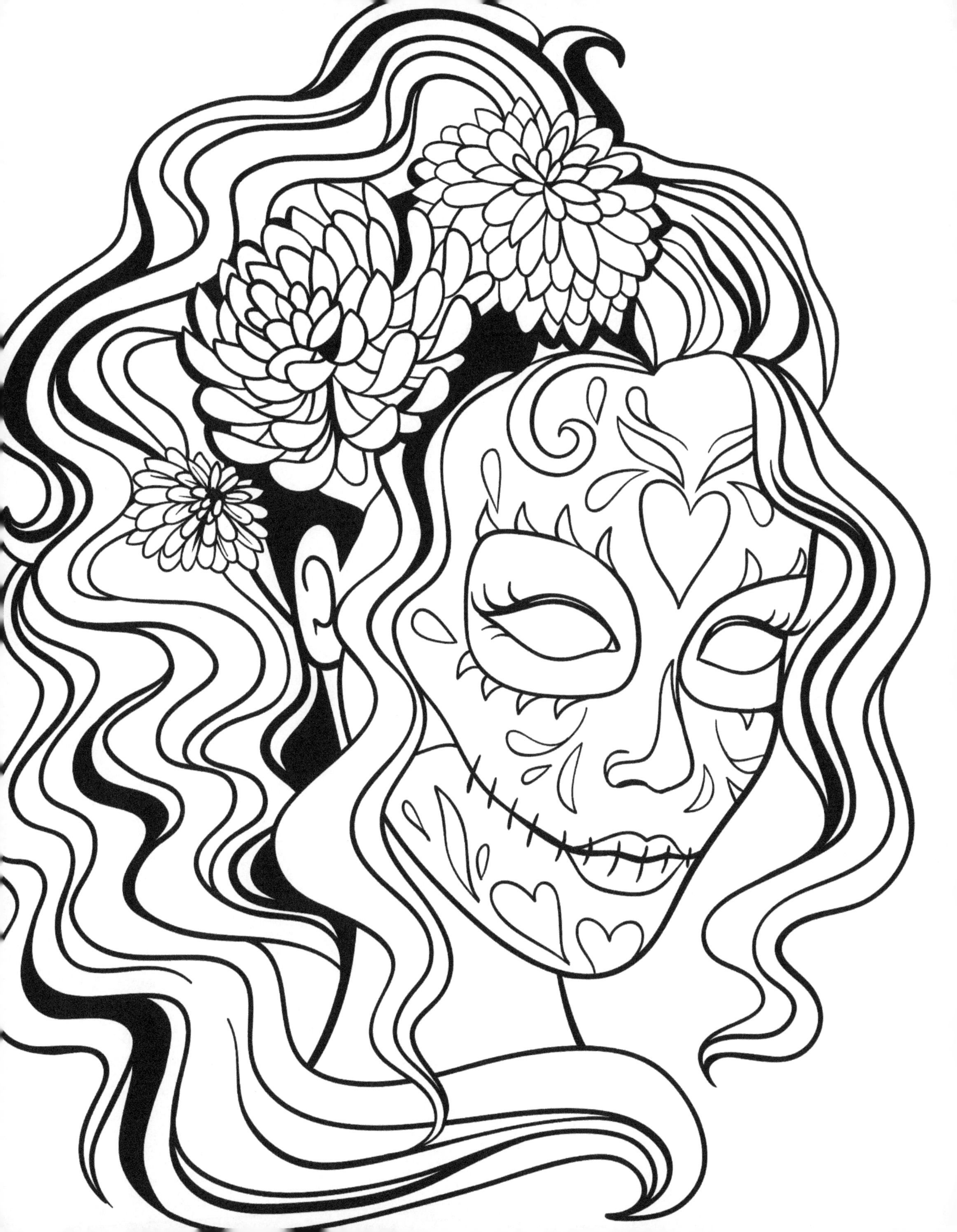

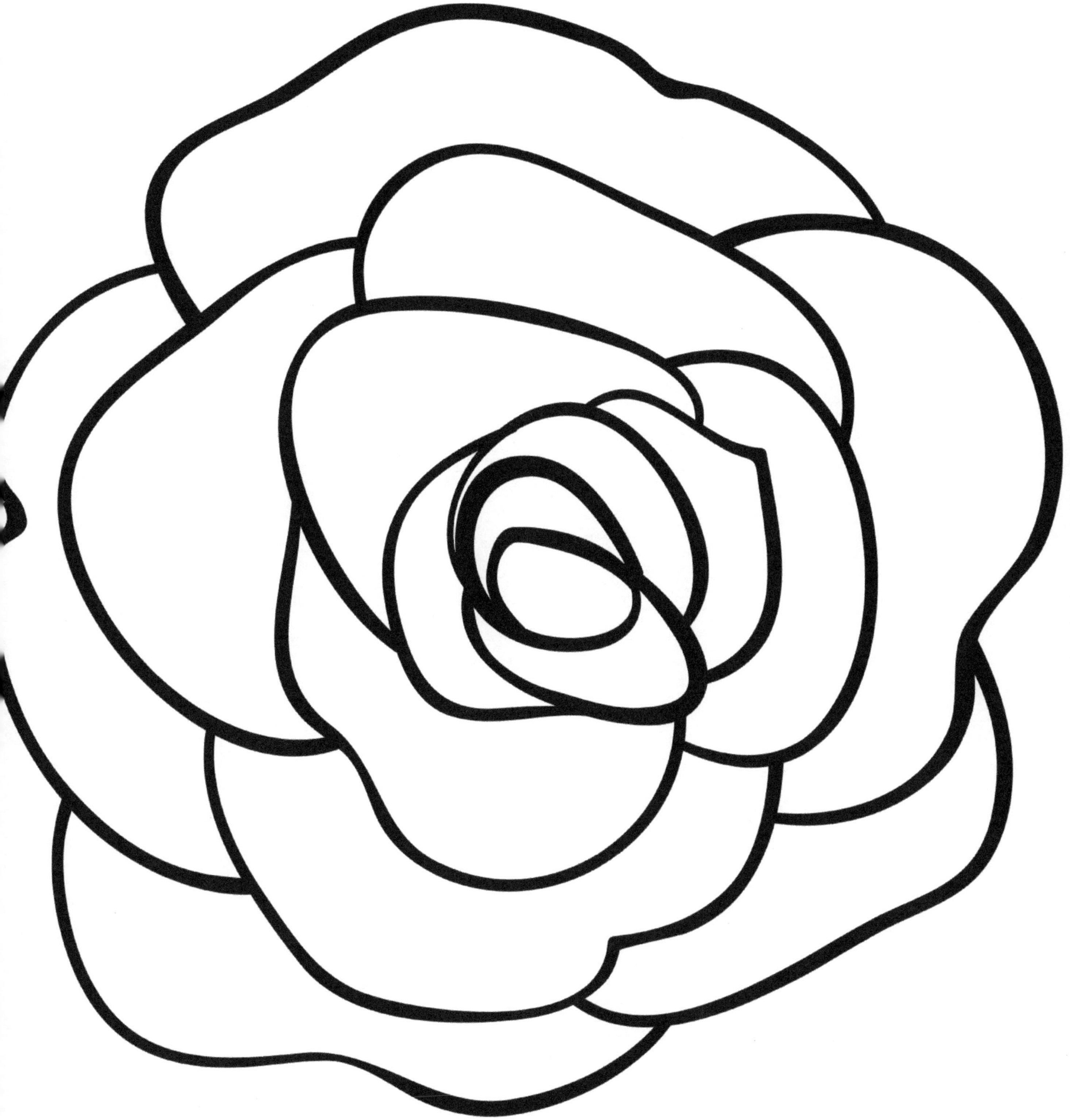

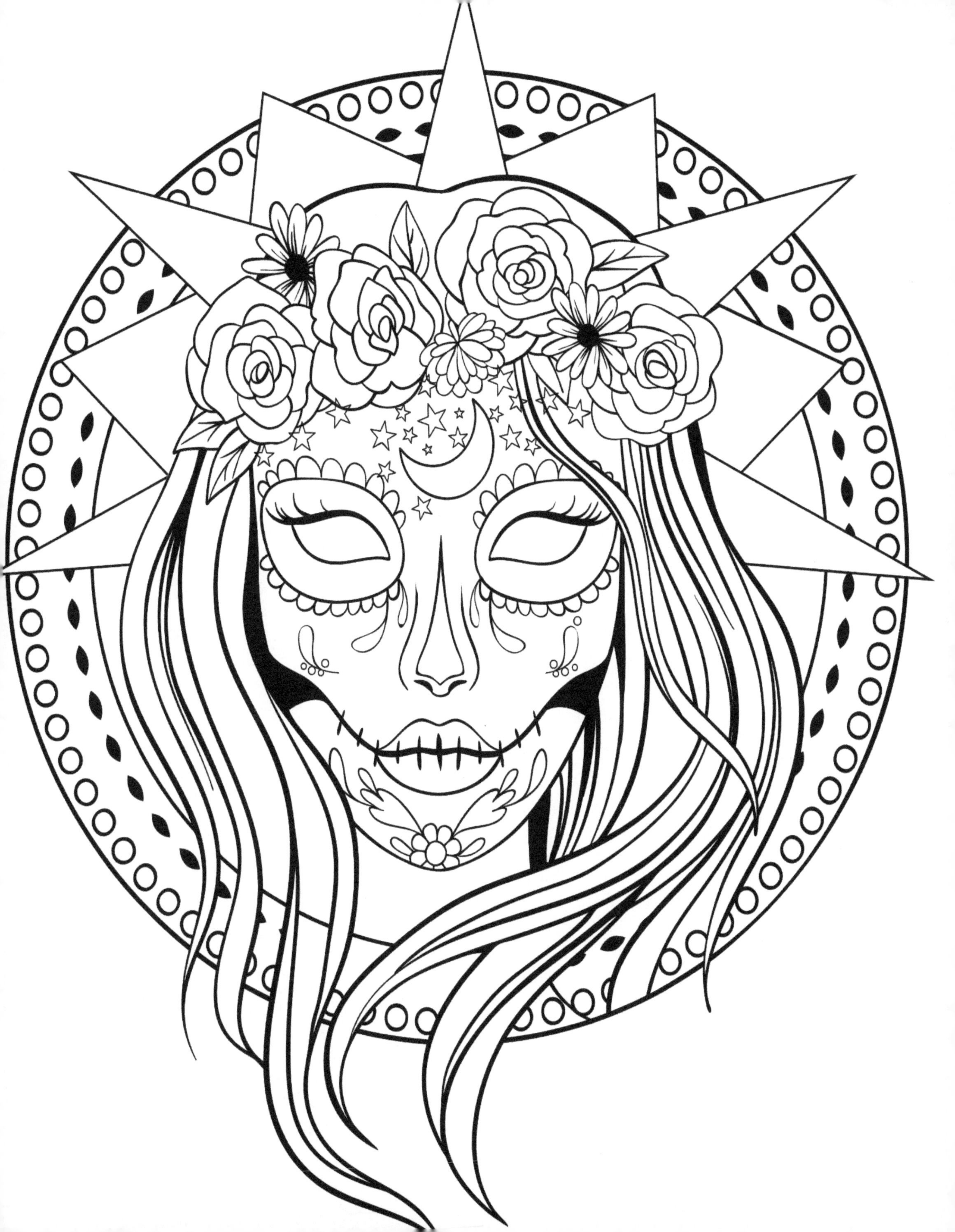

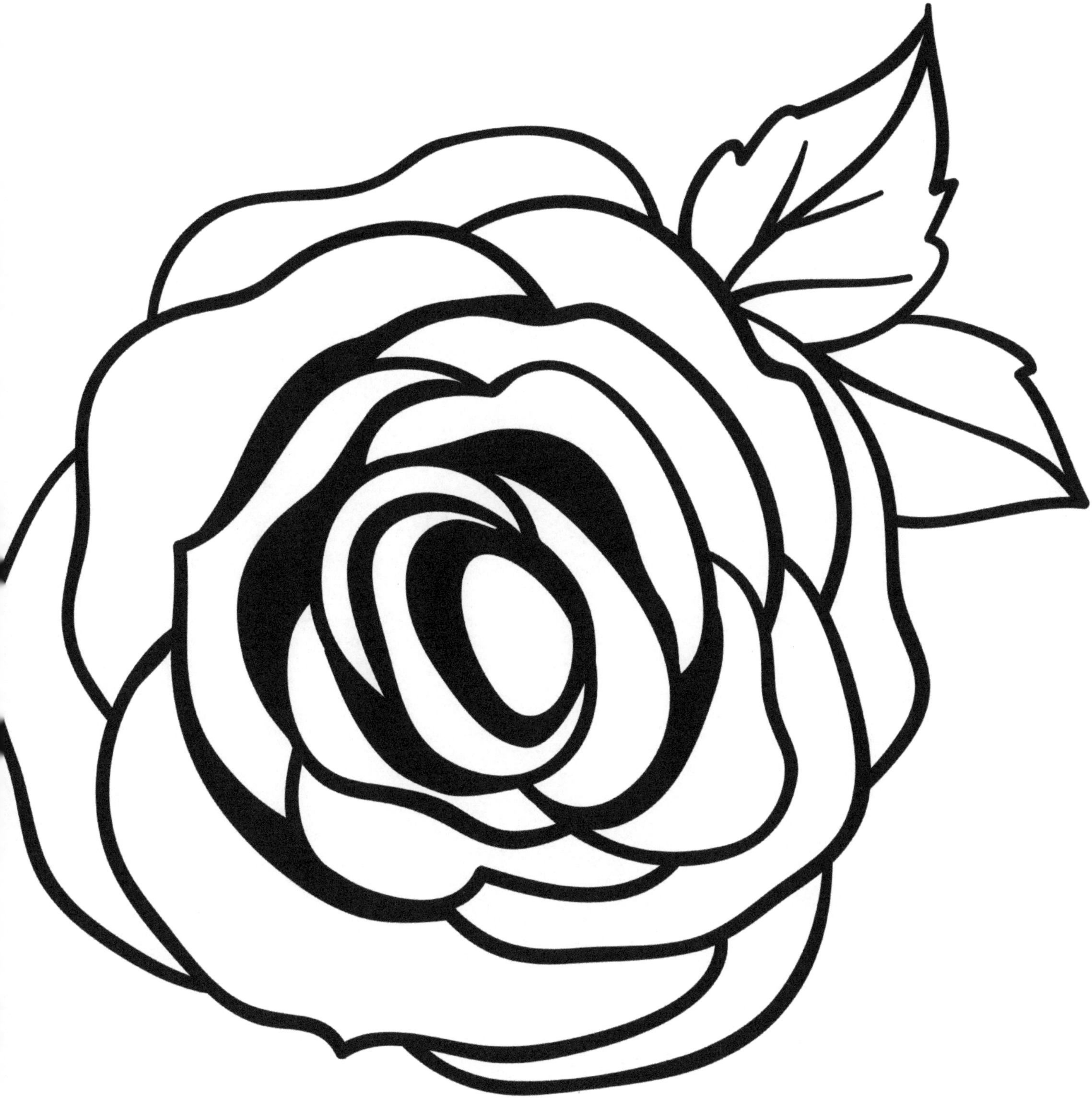

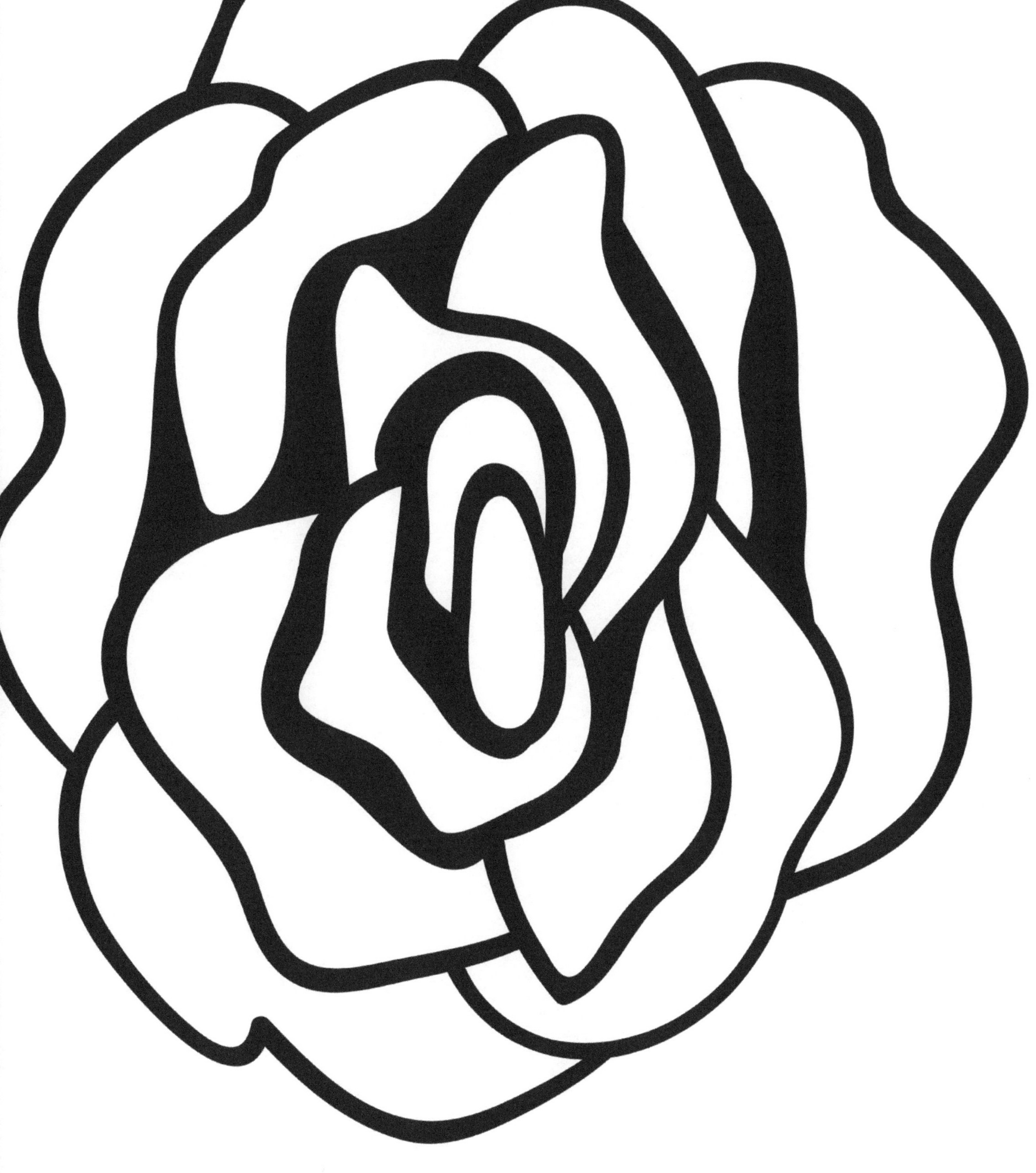

Lightning Source UK Ltd.
Milton Keynes UK
UKHW051449270720
367241UK00011B/339